bright sky press
HOUSTON, TEXAS

2365 Rice Blvd., Suite 202
Houston, Texas 77005

ISBN: 978-1-939055-81-1

10   9   8   7   6   5   4   3   2   1

Library of Congress Cataloging-in-Publication Data on file with publisher.

Editorial Direction, Lucy Herring Chambers
Editor, Eva J. Freeburn
Design, Marla Y. Garcia

Printed in Canada through Friesens

Silly Shoes

Poems to make you smile

Lawson Gow

Illustrations by

Mike Guillory

bright sky press

HOUSTON, TEXAS

THE WORLD IS TOO SERIOUS

Put on your silly shoes, tie them up tight!
Now wiggle your toes—doesn't that feel right?

Pull up your socks all the way to your shins.
Let's fasten on our big goofy grins!

'Cause the world's gone too frowny, too grumpy and grouch,
It's got too much darnit, too much fooey and ouch

What it needs is more giggle, more tee-hee lemonade!
Let's douse it with a bright colored silly grenade!

They'll say that we're wacky, downright batty no doubt,
But we are the ones who've got it all figured out!

We'll deliver medicine made from grin, laugh and peace
But we're not quite like doctors, we're the happy police!

We'll battle this world that's too grim, bleak, and gray!
We're ambassadors of the smile—saving the day!

BOWLING WITH SUPERMAN

If a day with Superman was auctioned off, I'd be the highest bidder,
But after a couple of hours, I think I'd reconsider.

His x-ray vision would make card games not so very fun,
In pick-up baseball, every pitch he'd crush a huge homerun.

I think he'd feel silly jumping on my trampoline,
And *I know* I'd feel silly being HIM for Halloween!

He's faster than a bullet and can stop a moving train,
So playing tag or sports with him? Borderline insane!

I think it would be hard for me and Superman to play,
Perhaps we'd all be better off if he just saves the day!

EXPRESSION FRUIT SALAD

Imagine an expression fruit salad
Made from all the things we say
All mixed and tossed together
In a colorful display.

We'd say *he went bananas*
And throw it in the pot.
We'd slice some *you're a peach*
And pit *I plumb forgot*.

We'd add some *cherry-picking*,
And to drink? We'd say,
*When life gives you lemons
Make some lemonade!*

BUT APPLES ARE THE BUSIEST FRUITS

Apples are too busy
They have no time for fun.
"We're ubiquitous!" they whine,
"There's too much to be done!"

Apples are like other fruits
And often eaten whole,
But also eaten as a pie
Or saucy in a bowl.

Sometimes they're sliced in halves
Where peanut butter's spread,
And must be at the ready
To be drank as juice instead.

We busy apples with our words
We give them much to chew,
It's all the stuff we say
That makes them a superfruit!

They have to be here everyday
To keep the doctors gone,
And think of all the teacher's desks
They must be sitting on?!

The big ones travel to New York
While others are preparing,
To be used in expression
With oranges for comparing.

So when you eat and speak of them
Your busy apple neighbor,
Just pause and appreciate
The fruits of the apple's labor.

MY CHOCOLATE BUNNY

One day my chocolate bunny,
As if in a trance,
Glanced up at me and said "Hi Pete!"
Then stood and did a dance!

I cheered "Yippee, hurray, yahoo!"
And watched him twist and bend,
And I knew when he smiled at me
That this guy was my friend

I dressed him up in people clothes
And pushed him in my sled.
Every night we'd read a book,
Then snuggle up in bed.

One night I grabbed a story
I was sure he'd like a lot
"Charlie's Chocolate Factory!"
Then I described the plot.

But as I read the book
His response, to my surprise,
Was just a distant, forlorn gaze
As chocolate milk welled in his eyes.

I stopped, concerned, and said to him,
"Hey buddy why so glum?"
He said, "That place in your book,
It's my home, that's where I'm from."

He wiped his chocolate milk-smeared cheeks
Looked up and said, "Hey Pete?
I miss my home a lot," he sniffed,
Shuffling his bunny feet.

I said "I understand and
You've been gone for much too long!
You're my best friend bunny,
But your home's where you belong."
We cried and hugged and said goodbyes
And as he hopped away,
I knew that though it hurt right now
The pain would melt away.

My friends, when things start to look bad,
Remember all the stuff that brings us our glad!

Like a baby dressed up in a pumpkin costume, or
When the zoo gives out free SpongeBob balloons.

When your luggage comes first down the baggage claim chute,
Or when at last from your teeth you free the dried fruit

Cold pillows, and undies worn straight from the dryer,
Onion rings eaten right out of the fryer

The smell of fireworks and a new Christmas tree,
Melon Starbursts and ginger green tea!

When your ice cream is gone and you're sad and distraught,
Look down in your bowl and drink the sweet melty glop!

Life is *not* such a serious race—
It doesn't need runners with stern on their face.

It's meant to be dorky danced and silly skipped,
To be goofy galloped, fool flipped and slipped!

Don't just run the race, confetti it too!
Don't steady your pace, bonanza on through!!

SMILE AMMO

A SNEEZE SANDWICH

One day Carl came to lunch
He'd brought a special treat
He said it was a sandwich
That he couldn't wait to eat

It didn't look that great—
Just some goo between the bread.
He offered me a bite,
But I stuck to mine instead.

'Cause as long as I've known Carl
He's been a little kooky-brained,
And I couldn't be too sure
About what Carl's snack contained.

I watched him for a while—
Oh how happily he munched.
So finally I asked him,
"Carl, what'd you bring for lunch?"

"A sneeze sandwich," he replied,
"It's made with bread and sneeze."
"Gross!" I yelled, but he just grinned,
"Could you pass the ketchup please?"

But as he chewed away
At his sneezy sandwich paste,
He made it look so good
I said, "Fine, give me a taste."

HAVING TO PEE IN PUBLIC

The worst thing about public and bladders:
When your bladder's full, nothing else matters.
At the risk of mean chants,
You'll go right in your pants,
Then you're stuck with the wet pee-pee splatters.

IF YOU THINK ABOUT HER TEETH

If something reminds you of her teeth
You've moved beyond a crush
Assume it's love when thoughts pop up
And instantly you gush

And if you talk about her toes
Then here's a truth you can't dispute
You, my friend, have got it BAD
When you think her toes are *cute*

If a girl walks in the room
And your buddies start to stare
You know that your heart's taken
If you don't look or even care

If she sneezes on the phone
When you're on the other line
And you start grinning ear to ear
That's a pretty darn good sign

If every song suddenly
Makes sense and speaks her name
If her picture makes your heart race:
You've failed to sidestep Cupid's aim

If every kiss is perfect
If you always want one more
Congrats my friend, you've found the thing
We all are looking for

A FLESHY GROWTH

If an alien looked at an ear
Its purpose would be quite unclear
"Give that weird growth a snip!"
He'd say, and we'd quip:
"No thanks, that's how I hear!"

A MEAL OF COLORS

I've got a special gift:
I can eat a meal of blue!
And chomp down on a nice big red
And slurp up bright orange stew!

I feast upon a juicy teal
And have some beige for snack.
I sip some pink, and yellow too
And crunch on jade and black.

I nibble on some burgundy,
And every afternoon
I wash down lunch with a glass
Of dark brown and maroon.

I can make a sandwich
From cyan and gooey gold—
These colors are the best because
They never rot or mold!

I can open up some indigo
That's kept fresh in a can
And chew on ruby like it's gum
No color's ever bland!

Neon colors can be sour,
Pastels, more light and sweet,
Fluorescent ones are often rich
And QUITE a tasty treat.

I hope the best restaurants
Will put on their display
A hot magenta casserole
And a taupe and mauve buffet!

Now that color's what I eat
I barbeque citrine,
And if the scarlet makes me fat,
I diet with light green.

Purple gets stuck between my teeth,
Chartreuse can make a mess,
And I'm careful when I'm eating bronze
Not to spill it on my dress!

Usually a little salt
Is what a crimson needs.
With lavender I make quite sure
I spit out ALL the seeds.

A smoothie made of turquoise
And a scoop of aged khaki,
Can be blended into a drink
That's oh so good for me!

With this special gift I've got
I see a rainbow in all I chew,
And not only can I see it—
But I can taste it, too!

BACKWARDS LAND

What's it like in backwards land?
To myself I often wonder
Is a storm a sunny day?
Would it have a flash of thunder?

I think I'd be confused
Gazing at a sky of red
And I *know* it would be strange to see
People walking on their heads!

Even the simplest things
Would be wacky, odd and eerie
You'd long for normal stuff again
The weird world would make you weary

If you saw a vending machine
"Hurray for normal!" you would cry
But when you took a closer look
You'd groan a fed-up sigh

For the Twizzlers would be crunchy!
Potato chips baked in a cake!
The Fig Newtons would be sour!
And the Twix served with a steak!

Nutterbutters now a liquid
That you drink right from the can!
Doritos now a frozen treat!
The gum fried in a pan!

The Snickers might be hollow!
Oh, what a disgrace!
The Reese's might be inside out!
What an awful awful place!

No, I couldn't handle
 Backwards stuff in backwards land.
Backwards candy is a thing
I know I simply could NOT stand!

THE POEM KILLER

In poetry, from time to time
You use a word that has no rhyme.

It stops the poem in its tracks
Because a rhyming match it lacks.

While plum, grape and clementine
In a line are often fine,

And cherry, apricot and date
Also tend to work out great,

And even guava and lychee
Are seen in rhyme quite frequently.

But if in writing you recruit
the deadly rhyme-void citrus fruit...

As a poet just resign—
You've just scribbled your last line:

'Cause *nothing* rhymes with orange.

HOW MUCH I LOVE YOU

Mom grounds me and I'm grumpy.
She says, "I love you." I say "LIES!"
"Not good enough?" she says,
"Then try THIS on for size—

If a lion came into your room
To make a snack of you,
I'd stand in front and say, Hey Lion!
I'm a bigger chew!"

And if you hurt your leg
A hundred thousand miles away,
I'd run each and every mile
And make sure that you're ok.

And if one night you're scared
Of the monsters in your room,
I'll stand guard all night long
Armed and ready with my broom.

And I'm the one, when you're asleep,
Who creeps in with tiptoed feet
To lay my head against your heart
Just to listen to its beat.

And I'm the one who held you first
And won't forget the day
I heard you blurt out your first word:
It was "Mom" you chose to say.

I'M GLAD FOR BELLY BUTTONS

I'm glad I have a belly button—
That divot in my tummy.
I imagine if my eyes were there,
They'd make seeing rather crummy.

I'd always have to lift my shirt
Just to look around,
And were my ears beneath my shirt
I'd hear a muffled sound.

And if my nose were there instead,
Tight hugs might hurt a bit.
If I sneezed just IMAGINE
The weird looks that I would get!

Oh how very glad I am
My belly button's in its place,
Can you imagine if instead we had
Belly buttons on our face?!

COUGH IN MY FACE

What if sickness had good symptoms?
Would it still be called *disease?*
If someone said, "Want to get sick?"
Would you say, "Oh, yes please?!"

What if sickness had good symptoms?
If sore throats didn't cause any pain?
Would you let folks cough in your face?
You'd welcome the itch and strain!

Would the best colds be contagious?
You could spread illness like it were cheer!
Instead of ostracizing sick
We'd say, "You there, please come near!"

"Please stand real close to me!"
We'd say, and, "Hey, sneeze on my food!"
And if some sick guy didn't share,
You'd say, "Man that guy's rude!"

If being sick felt good,
Docs would lose their jobs.
Trash cans would be full of meds
And ointments, creams and swabs.

And what if injury felt good?
You broke your arm? "Who cares?!" You'd say!
X-rays, casts, and surgery—
Those things would go away!

LIFE'S COLORS

Now look here you swashbuckler!
Look here petulant crank!
You're irritable and grouchy—
Time to fill your cheerful tank!

The fix should be so easy,
It's those dark shades you wear—
They've darkened, dulled and faded
All the colors out there!

There's vibrance you see,
That your dark shades have hid
When you're looking at
The world in gray grid!

Those shades tint your days
And they have you forgetting,
All the good stuff—
It's only sketches you're getting!

Your eyes see the world now
As no one prefers,
Just tracings and outlines—
Just sparkle-less blurs!

Take them off! Take them off!
There's life's brightness to see!
There are splashes of colors—
Look at them shades free!

THE LOST WORLD
(NOT THE DINOSAUR ONE)

They all live together
(the forgotten toys I mean)
On some hidden land among us
Where they're rarely ever seen

But what makes toys go to this place?
It's when they're left behind
When their kids don't want them anymore
They move out of sight and mind

Here they retire with old friends
And talk about the days
When THEY were what kids had to have—
Alas, fame never sticks or stays

The Beanie Babies are in charge
They govern all the land
Princess Diana (as you'd expect)
Is first in command

The Game Boys and the Digimon
Often play together
It's safer for them in this place
(There's never rainy weather)

The Tickle-Me Elmoes and the Furbies
Get along quite well
Their kindness got scared Pokemon
To come out of their shells

But this place is far from perfect
As every Cabbage Patch Kid knows
A gang of mean toys roam the streets
And day by day it grows

The gang was formed by X-Brain yo-yo's
And rough-around-the-edges Pogs
The riff-raff has a gang house
Built with shanty Lincoln Logs

To rid her land of the gang
Diana hired pros
A special team to catch them
Made of fourteen GI Joes

But overall this land is nice
For forgotten toys to move on
If you've lost one, don't worry:
It's HERE your toy has gone

THE OLD TRAMPOLINE FINALLY SNAPS

There once was an old trampoline
Who was sick of the same old routine

So he pinned down poor Shelly
And bounced on *her* belly

And yelled, "You see what I mean?!"

THE MALICIOUS PAIR of JEANS

Mitch got sucked into his jeans
Right before our eyes.
This is the story of poor
Mitchell Ericson's demise.

Like all great epic truthful tales,
This one starts and ends with gum.
But unlike most great tales,
This one's first word was "Umm."

"Umm," said Mitch, "I think I'll have
The blue blast bubble kind."
With this purchase, though,
Mitch's life started to unwind.

'Cause Mitch's jeans on this day
Were particularly malicious
And, unlike Mitch, found the gum
To be not quite so delicious.

So when Mitch jammed his pockets
Full of blue blast flavored gum,
The malicious pair of jeans
Quickly grabbed his thumb.

The jeans kept tugging 'til
They had pulled in Mitch's arm,
And we just watched, frozen stiff
In petrified alarm.

Mitch, now shoulder deep,
Tried to yank his body free
He screamed out, *"Help!*
My jeans are eating me!"

What could we do? We watched
Until poor Mitchell was no more.
Just a pair of jeans, two shoes,
And the gum lay on the floor.

I'M GLAD
I'M A BOY

There are things I'm glad I'm not:
Like a plant stuck in a pot

Or a nose hair in a sneeze
Or a stinky piece of cheese

Or chewed up gum stuck on a shoe
Or an injured Kangaroo

Or a font that no one uses
Or a scab with pus that oozes

Or a girl named Avocado
Or poop-flavored gelato

Or a peach left in the sun,
That's no fun for anyone.

But I'm a boy, these things I'm not—
And I lucked out with what I got!

AMBASSADOR ARMOR

Remember now gang, there's angry out there.
If we fight unprepared—we won't have a prayer.

With goof in our hearts and glee in our grins
We must put on armor for the battle begins,

The uniform of the wacky with Elmo-rimmed glasses
To spread smile throughout the cantankerous masses.

So put on your sweater of happy-go-lucky
To protect against serious, buzz-kill and yucky!

Put on giggle jean shorts, make sure that they're snug.
They'll protect you from the bites of the negative bug.

Remember to sharpen your friendship-sword blades,
And make sure that you've got plenty silly grenades.

We're ready now gang, let's go stomp out the pout!
And show this world what loving life's all about!

PUT ON YOUR
SILLY SHOES AND TIE
THEM UP TIGHT!